Supplement to

Building

Continual

Improvement

Chapter Thirteen
Version 2.0

Donald J. Wheeler

Sheila R. Poling

SPC Press

Knoxville, Tennessee

Preface

In the original version of Chapter Thirteen of Building Continual Improvement we presented a way of seasonally adjusting time-series data. The method we presented had the advantage that it avoided making an adjustment unless that adjustment would actually reduce the overall variation of the time series. Since the primary objective of seasonal adjustment is the removal of systematic variation, this feature of our method seemed reasonable. Moreover, given the huge reductions in variation that could be achieved by deseasonalization, it did not seem to be worthwhile to include adjustments for effects which would generally have a smaller impact upon the variation.

However, in the case of the seasonal adjustment of time-series data the effects that we overlooked were not as small as we originally thought. With growing usage we became aware of some problems with our original procedure for deseasonalization of a time series.

As we investigated these problems we became convinced of the necessity of modifying our approach. We needed to modify the way we defined the seasonal factors, and we needed to modify the way we computed limits for deseasonalized future values. These modifications to the original procedure are included in this new version of Chapter Thirteen. They have the virtue of being sounder from a theoretical viewpoint while resulting in a procedure that is actually less complex than the original version. We are indebted to Dr. Roger Sym and Brian Wood for the role they played as a catalyst in bringing about this improvement.

Chapter Thirteen

Version 2.0

Seasonal Data

Many time series display regular seasonal patterns and trends. These patterns and trends can be useful in your analysis and understanding of the data, but they also may obscure signals of changes which you would like to detect. Therefore, in order to get the most out of your data, you may need to be able to work with seasonal patterns and trends. Chapter Nine showed how to construct simple trend lines and trended limits for a time-series plot. In this chapter we will outline some ways of working with data which display seasonal patterns. Of course, the use of the term "seasonal" does not restrict us to working with quarterly data. Seasonality is a label for any regularly recurring pattern in a time series.

13.1 Moving Averages

Perhaps the simplest way to handle seasonal patterns is to average or smooth them out. Figure 12.9, on page 212, shows data with a pattern that repeats itself every week. In Exercise 12.3 the weekly averages for these data were plotted on an *XmR* chart, revealing the underlying trend without the clutter of the weekly pattern. But this method has the disadvantage of requiring that you wait until the end of the week to plot a point. While this may not represent too great an inconvenience with weekly data, it can become a problem with annual patterns—we do not want to wait until the end of the year to see how we are doing.

A second way of removing a seasonal pattern is to use a year-long *moving average*. With quarterly data, a four-period moving average will always contain four quarters worth of data, and therefore will average out the seasonal effects to reveal the underlying average. (With monthly values a year-long moving average would become a twelve-point moving average.)

To illustrate a moving average we will begin with the quarterly sales values from Region C, shown in Table 13.1. To compute a four-period moving average you obtain the sum of each successive group of four periods. The sum of the sales for the first four periods is 4306. The sum for Periods 2, 3, 4 and 5 is 4407. The sum for Periods 3, 4, 5, and 6 is 4505, etc.

Table 13.1: Quarterly Sales for Region C

Year	Quarter	Period	Region C Sales	4-Period Sum	4-Period Moving Average
One	I	1	1056	—	—
	II	2	1048	—	—
	III	3	1129	—	—
	IV	4	1073	4306	1076.50
Two	I	5	1157	4407	1101.75
	II	6	1146	4505	1126.25
	III	7	1064	4440	1110.00
	IV	8	1213	4580	1145.00
Three	I	9	1088	4511	1127.75
	II	10	1322	4687	1171.75
	III	11	1256	4879	1219.75
	IV	12	1132	4798	1199.50
Four	I	13	1352	5062	1265.50
	II	14	1353	5093	1273.25
	III	15	1466	5303	1325.75
	IV	16	1196	5367	1341.75
Five	I	17	1330	5345	1336.25
	II	18	1003	4995	1248.75
	III	19	1197	4726	1181.50
	IV	20	1337	4867	1216.75

Next you divide each of the four-period sums by 4.0 to obtain the four-period moving averages shown in the last column of Table 13.1. While a moving average is not hard to compute, the computations can become tedious, which is where modern spreadsheet programs become useful. Figure 13.1 combines the individual values with the four-period moving average for Region C.

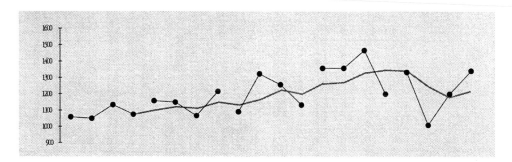

Figure 13.1: Sales for Region C and Four-Period Moving Average

The plot shown in Figure 13.1 is a very powerful summary. The individual values show the levels for each month, allowing you to look for seasonal patterns and abnormal events. At the same time the four-period moving average removes any seasonality that might be present. It also removes the month-to-month noise that complicates the interpretation of the individual values. The four-period moving average reveals the long-term trends in a way that is simple and easy to interpret. This estimate of the trend is automatically updated every time you compute the moving average. And the latest value of the moving average provides you with an instantaneous estimate of current sales levels, after making allowance for recent trends and removing seasonal influences. Finally, the four-period moving average provides a balanced view of the sales levels without being unduly influenced by the euphoria of a good quarter or the depression of a bad quarter.

For those measures that are merely report card measures it is hard to do better than to plot them in the format of Figure 13.1.

Moving averages are a way to smooth the data. They provide a floating central line for the plot in Figure 13.1. When you use a moving average you are characterizing the trend rather than looking for signals. In most cases, little will be gained by computing limits for a year-long moving average.

The moving average is sometimes said to lag behind the time-series. This is because any moving average is constructed using historical values. We computed the first value of the four-period moving average at Time Period 4, and this is where we plotted it in Figure 13.1. In truth, the first value for the four-period moving average is the average for Time Periods 1, 2, 3, and 4, and might more properly be plotted at the mid-point of these four time periods, (Time Period 2.5). When this is done in Figure 13.1, it has the effect of shifting the moving average curve back 1.5 time periods. This shifted curve is shown in Figure 13.2, along with the trended limits found (back in Chapter 9) using the first four years of values. Notice how closely the shifted four-period moving average matches the trend line during Years One to Four.

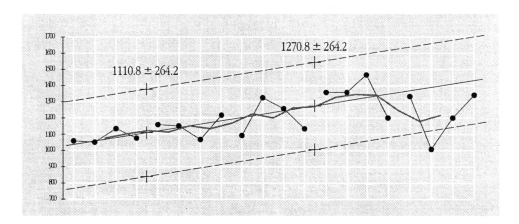

Figure 13.2: Sales for Region C and Four-Period Moving Average

To illustrate a 12-period moving average we will use the data from Table 13.2.

Table 13.2: Monthly Boutique Sales

Year	J	F	M	A	M	J	J	A	S	O	N	D
One	15.0	23.3	35.6	35.0	51.1	50.7	45.6	52.0	46.8	48.2	70.5	96.6
Two	20.1	17.6	23.9	44.9	72.2	59.1	48.5	66.7	42.3	60.2	82.4	141.2
Three	19.0	28.8	35.6	48.1	63.8	49.3	45.6	52.2	46.1	72.9	98.4	122.1

Table 13.3: 12-Period Moving Average for Boutique Sales

Time Period	Values Used (12-period moving subgroups)												Moving Average
12	15.0	23.3	35.6	35.0	51.1	50.7	45.6	52.0	46.8	48.2	70.5	**96.6**	**47.53**
13	23.3	35.6	35.0	51.1	50.7	45.6	52.0	46.8	48.2	70.5	**96.6**	20.1	47.96
14	35.6	35.0	51.1	50.7	45.6	52.0	46.8	48.2	70.5	**96.6**	20.1	17.6	47.48
15	35.0	51.1	50.7	45.6	52.0	46.8	48.2	70.5	**96.6**	20.1	17.6	23.9	46.51
16	51.1	50.7	45.6	52.0	46.8	48.2	70.5	**96.6**	20.1	17.6	23.9	44.9	47.33
17	50.7	45.6	52.0	46.8	48.2	70.5	**96.6**	20.1	17.6	23.9	44.9	72.2	49.09
18	45.6	52.0	46.8	48.2	70.5	**96.6**	20.1	17.6	23.9	44.9	72.2	59.1	49.79
19	52.0	46.8	48.2	70.5	**96.6**	20.1	17.6	23.9	44.9	72.2	59.1	48.5	50.03
20	46.8	48.2	70.5	**96.6**	20.1	17.6	23.9	44.9	72.2	59.1	48.5	66.7	51.26
21	48.2	70.5	**96.6**	20.1	17.6	23.9	44.9	72.2	59.1	48.5	66.7	42.3	50.88
22	70.5	**96.6**	20.1	17.6	23.9	44.9	72.2	59.1	48.5	66.7	42.3	60.2	51.88
23	**96.6**	20.1	17.6	23.9	44.9	72.2	59.1	48.5	66.7	42.3	60.2	82.4	52.88
24	20.1	17.6	23.9	44.9	72.2	59.1	48.5	66.7	42.3	60.2	82.4	**141.2**	**56.59**
25	17.6	23.9	44.9	72.2	59.1	48.5	66.7	42.3	60.2	82.4	**141.2**	19.0	56.50
26	23.9	44.9	72.2	59.1	48.5	66.7	42.3	60.2	82.4	**141.2**	19.0	28.8	57.43
27	44.9	72.2	59.1	48.5	66.7	42.3	60.2	82.4	**141.2**	19.0	28.8	35.6	58.41
28	72.2	59.1	48.5	66.7	42.3	60.2	82.4	**141.2**	19.0	28.8	35.6	48.1	58.68
29	59.1	48.5	66.7	42.3	60.2	82.4	**141.2**	19.0	28.8	35.6	48.1	63.8	57.98
30	48.5	66.7	42.3	60.2	82.4	**141.2**	19.0	28.8	35.6	48.1	63.8	49.3	57.16
31	66.7	42.3	60.2	82.4	**141.2**	19.0	28.8	35.6	48.1	63.8	49.3	45.6	56.92
32	42.3	60.2	82.4	**141.2**	19.0	28.8	35.6	48.1	63.8	49.3	45.6	52.2	55.71
33	60.2	82.4	**141.2**	19.0	28.8	35.6	48.1	63.8	49.3	45.6	52.2	46.1	56.03
34	82.4	**141.2**	19.0	28.8	35.6	48.1	63.8	49.3	45.6	52.2	46.1	72.9	57.08
35	**141.2**	19.0	28.8	35.6	48.1	63.8	49.3	45.6	52.2	46.1	72.9	98.4	58.42
36	19.0	28.8	35.6	48.1	63.8	49.3	45.6	52.2	46.1	72.9	98.4	**122.1**	**56.83**

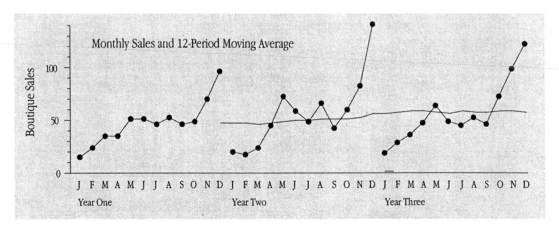

Figure 13.3: Boutique Sales and 12-Period Moving Average

The 12-period moving average is found by computing the average for each successive group of 12 values, as shown in Table 13.3. Since it will take 12 values to get started, the first value is computed at the 12th time period. Thus we get 25 moving averages from the 36 monthly values above. Figure 13.3 shows the monthly sales and the moving averages.

While the monthly values show the pronounced seasonality of the boutique sales, the moving averages in Figure 13.3 remove these seasonal effects and show a gradual upward trend in sales. The current value of the moving average can always be converted into an annual sales amount by multiplying by 12. For example, the last value of 56.83 converts into total sales for the past 12 months of approximately 682 thousand dollars.

The advantages of combining a year-long moving average with the time-series plot of the individual values are simplicity, accessibility, and interpretability. The information contained in the data is conveyed to your readers with a minimum of fuss, with a minimum of effort, and without distracting details. For report card measures, this simple graph will often be sufficient.

As an additional example Figure 13.4 shows the Daily Department Store Sales values from Table 12.3, page 211, with a 7-point moving average superimposed. The breaks in the running record provide anchor points for your eye so that you can see each week's values and the pattern within each week. The 7-point moving average removes this weekly pattern and provides a floating central line which serves to show the overall trend in these sales values. While the daily sales vary from 4,000 to 19,000, the average can be seen to have edged up slightly from just below 9,000 to just below 10,000 during this 13 week period.

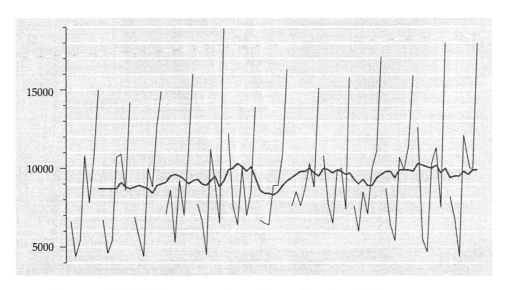

Figure 13.4: Daily Department Store Sales and a 7-Period Moving Average

The one drawback to a n-period moving average is its tendency to show n-period cycles. This phenomenon can be seen in Figure 13.4. The excessively high sales on the last day of Week 5 and the first day of Week 6 each affect the next seven moving averages, creating the upswing in the moving average seen in Week 6. In the same way, the lower sales on the following weekend (the end of Week 6 and the beginning of Week 7) create the "recession" seen in Week 7. Exceptionally large or exceptionally small values will always influence the moving average for the next n-periods, and will give rise to these spurious cycles. The user should therefore refrain from interpreting an n-period cycle as a change in the underlying system until after checking to see if it is due to one or two extreme values.

13.2 Year-to-Date Plots

The problems of noise in the data and of seasonal effects have been appreciated for a long time. What has been lacking is an appreciation of the effective ways of handling these problems in an understandable and straightforward manner. The year-long moving average superimposed on a plot of the individual values, as described in the previous section, is an effective way of dealing with both noise and seasonal effects. Moreover, it is far superior to the more common practice of plotting the year-to-date values.

Table 13.4: Appliance Store Sales

Monthly Sales

Year	J	F	M	A	M	J	J	A	S	O	N	D
One	86.9	78.3	97.2	77.3	113.5	99.5	75.0	81.8	113.4	122.3	74.4	80.4
Two	72.3	78.1	91.5	91.7	141.5	113.2	107.0	96.7	99.1	71.8	78.4	46.5

Twelve-Period Moving Averages

Year	J	F	M	A	M	J	J	A	S	O	N	D
One												91.7
Two	90.5	90.4	90.0	91.1	93.5	94.6	97.3	98.5	97.4	93.1	93.5	90.7

Year-to-Date Values

Year	J	F	M	A	M	J	J	A	S	O	N	D
One	87	165	262	340	453	553	628	710	823	945	1020	1100
Two	72	150	242	334	475	588	695	792	891	963	1041	1088

The first problem with year-to-date values is the naive comparisons which they encourage. For example, consider the year-to-date values for Year Two above. In January it is reported that sales are lagging behind last year's sales. They are behind in February. They are behind in March. They are still behind in April. What a disaster! But wait, in May they pull ahead of last year's sales level and the gloom is dispelled. They are ahead in June. They are ahead in July. They are ahead in August. What a great year! They are ahead in September. They are ahead in October. They are ahead in November. And yet they finish the year behind last year—so kiss the bonus good-bye. And that is how year-to-date values are one of the major causes of man-made chaos. Whether we look at the year-to-date plot or the year-to-date values in the table we end up making the same naive comparisons because that is all these values will allow.

The second problem with year-to-date values is that they do not provide a simple and direct way of estimating the overall level of sales. Yet the moving averages show the sales level to be averaging in the vicinity of 90 to 100 thousand per month.

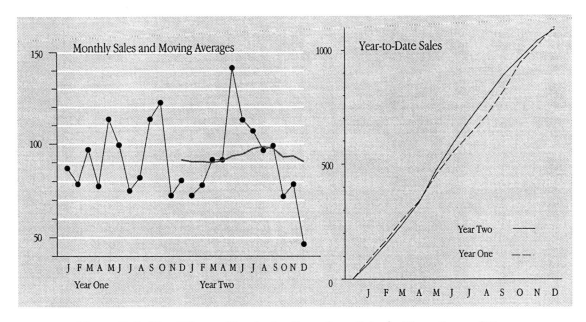

Figure 13.5: Two Ways to Plot the Appliance Store Sales for Years One and Two

The third problem with year-to-date values is that they do not easily provide an estimate of the annual sales. In contrast to this, at any point in time, the current moving average times 12 is equal to the total sales over the previous 12 months.

The fourth problem with the year-to-date plots is that they replace the "levels" of the plot on the left with the "slopes" on the right. Since slopes are much more subjective to interpret, and since the lines are seldom straight, this shift is one that introduces more complexity than clarity.

The fifth problem with year-to-date plots is that they require an extremely compressed scale. This happens because the vertical scale has to allow for the annual total. As a consequence, even big swings in monthly values will result in small changes in angle. For example, the spike in sales in May of Year Two is easy to see on the left, but hard to find on the right. And the dramatic drop in sales in December of Year Two is only a slight change in angle on the year-to-date plot. While it is good to smooth out noise, the compressed scale of the year-to-date plot tends to obliterate more than just the noise.

So year-to-date values will tell you that "when you're up you're up, and when you're down you're down, but when you're only half-way up you're neither up nor down." The running record and year-long moving average plot will generally provide more useful information, in a more accessible format, than will year-to-date plots.

13.3 The Problem of Seasonal Effects

The year-long moving average hides seasonal effects by averaging them out. Another way of working with seasonal effects is to explicitly adjust the data to allow for seasonality.

To illustrate data that have a strong seasonal pattern which is recurring from year to year we shall look at the monthly sales figures for a single store in a chain of department stores. The monthly sales, in thousands of dollars, are shown in Table 13.5, and the time series plot for these data is shown in Figure 13.6.

Table 13.5: Monthly Department Store Sales

	J	F	M	A	M	J	J	A	S	O	N	D
Year One	242.5	295.1	377.9	330.6	425.0	395.3	384.3	415.8	380.8	447.9	525.0	566.6
Year Two	241.0	287.2	365.0	322.1	418.8	400.2	403.7	410.9	382.8	449.8	520.7	549.1
Year Three	252.4	309.5	405.1									

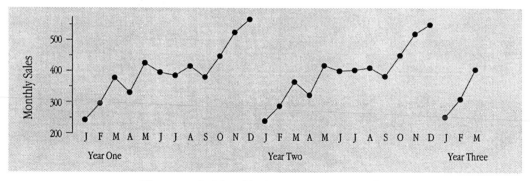

Figure 13.6: Monthly Department Store Sales

Clearly the dominant feature of the running record in Figure 13.6 is an annual pattern. This annual pattern effectively undermines simple comparisons between successive months—January cannot be compared with either December or February. So while we can use these data to compare January with January, and February with February, etc., we cannot compare months within a year.

If we should attempt to place these data on an *XmR* chart we would get something like Figure 13.7, which only reveals what we already knew—there is a detectable difference in sales volume from month to month throughout the year.

Now just how can the manager of this store interpret the sales for the First Quarter of Year Three? He has made changes in the store's advertising and he wants to know if it has had an impact. Can he use Figure 13.7 to tell if sales have changed? With the strong monthly pattern, and the large amount of month-to-month variation, it is difficult to make a reliable judgment using either Figure 13.6 or 13.7. We ought to be able to exploit the annual pattern to make our analysis more sensitive. And this is where deseasonalized data are helpful.

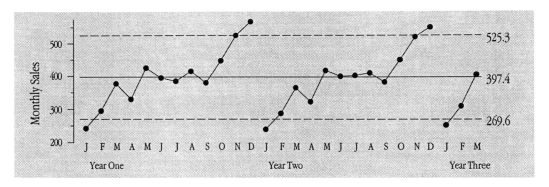

Figure 13.7: *X* Chart for Monthly Sales

13.4 Descasonalized Values

A value is deseasonalized by removing the average seasonal effect. (A way of determining the seasonal effects is outlined in the next section.) Deseasonalized monthly sales are obtained by dividing each monthly sales value by the corresponding seasonal factor.

$$\text{Deseasonalized Monthly Sales} \ = \ \frac{\text{Monthly Sales}}{\text{Seasonal Factor for that month}}$$

For the Department Store Sales, the actual sales for January of Year One are 242.5 thousand. However, as we will find in the next section, the sales in January are typically about 61% as big as the average monthly sales for the year:

(Average Monthly Sales for Year) x (0.61) = Average January Sales Value

So if we divide our current January Sales figure of 242.5 thousand by the January Seasonal Factor of 0.61 we will obtain an estimate of our average monthly sales for this year:

$$\frac{242.5 \text{ thousand}}{0.61} \ = \ 397.5 \text{ thousand}$$

Sales of 242.5 thousand in January are equivalent to an average monthly sales level of 397.5 thousand per month, or a annual sales level of:

12 x 397.5 thousand = $ 4,770,000

The actual sales for February of Year One were 295.1 thousand. In the past the sales in February have been about 73% of the average monthly sales for the year. Therefore, sales of 295.1 thousand in February are equivalent to an average monthly sales level of:

$$\frac{295.1 \text{ thousand}}{0.73} = 404.2 \text{ thousand}$$

Notice how the different sales values for January and February (242.5 and 295.1 differ by 18%) become quite similar when adjusted for seasonal effects (397.5 and 404.2 differ by 1.7%). Thus, a deseasonalized value (also known as a seasonally adjusted value) is one that has been converted into an estimated average value.

When you deseasonalize a set of values you are dividing those numbers that tend to be large by a large seasonal factor, and you are dividing those numbers that tend to be small by a small seasonal factor, with the result that "things even out" and the adjusted values may reasonably be compared. You may see this happening in Table 13.6 which contains: (1) the monthly sales, (2) the seasonal factors, and (3) the deseasonalized monthly sales for the Department Store Sales for Years One and Two.

Table 13.6: Deseasonalized Monthly Department Store Sales

	J	F	M	A	M	J	J	A	S	O	N	D
Yr One Monthly Sales	242.5	295.1	377.9	330.6	425.0	395.3	384.3	415.8	380.8	447.9	525.0	566.6
Seasonal Factors	0.61	0.73	0.93	0.82	1.06	1.00	1.00	1.04	0.96	1.13	1.32	1.40
Yr I Deseasonalized	397.5	404.2	406.3	403.2	400.9	395.3	384.3	399.8	396.7	396.3	397.7	404.7
Yr Two Monthly Sales	241.0	287.2	365.0	322.1	418.8	400.2	403.7	410.9	382.8	449.8	520.7	549.1
Seasonal Factors	0.61	0.73	0.93	0.82	1.06	1.00	1.00	1.04	0.96	1.13	1.32	1.40
Yr II Deseasonalized	395.1	393.4	392.5	392.8	395.1	400.2	403.7	395.1	398.8	398.1	394.5	392.2

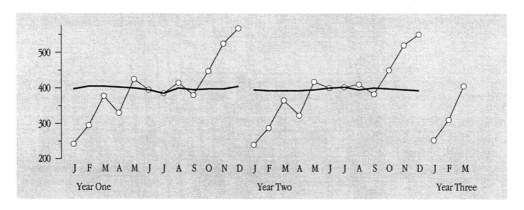

Figure 13.8: Monthly Sales and Deseasonalized Monthly Sales

Figure 13.8 shows the deseasonalized monthly sales superimposed upon the monthly sales. Clearly when you deseasonalize a time series you remove the average annual pattern. This allows you to look for other interesting signals which may be contained in the data. The vertical scale of Figure 13.8 is such that about all we can tell from the deseasonalized data is that they approximate the annual average for each year. To learn more from the deseasonalized data we will eventually place them on an *XmR* chart. But first we need to find our seasonal factors.

13.5 Finding Seasonal Factors

In computing seasonal factors you will need at least two years worth of data. Three or more years may be used, but since we are not interested in ancient history we will rarely need more than four or five years worth of data. We will illustrate this procedure using the department store sales for Years One and Two.

The first step in constructing seasonal factors is to compute the seasonal relatives for each season or month. This is done by dividing each month's value by the average value for that year—the value for January of Year One would be divided by the average monthly value for Year One, etc. In Year One the department store had sales of 4,786.8 thousand. This corresponds to a monthly average of 398.9 thousand. The January sales were 242.5 thousand. The seasonal relative for January of Year One is thus:

$$\text{Seasonal Relative} = \frac{\text{this month's value}}{\text{average monthly value}} = \frac{242.5 \text{ thousand}}{398.9 \text{ thousand}} = 0.608$$

Since we are only concerned with the approximate relationship between the monthly values and the annual average, it is unnecessary to record the seasonal relatives to more than three decimal places. The seasonal relatives for Years One and Two are shown in Table 13.7.

Table 13.7: Seasonal Relatives for the Department Store Sales

	J	F	M	A	M	J	J	A	S	O	N	D
Year One Sales	242.5	295.1	377.9	330.6	425.0	395.3	384.3	415.8	380.8	447.9	525.0	566.6
Average for Year 1	398.9	398.9	398.9	398.9	398.9	398.9	398.9	398.9	398.9	398.9	398.9	398.9
Seasonal Relatives	.608	.740	.947	.829	1.065	.991	.963	1.042	.955	1.123	1.316	1.420
Year Two Sales	241.0	287.2	365.0	322.1	418.8	400.2	403.7	410.9	382.8	449.8	520.7	549.1
Average for Year 2	395.9	395.9	395.9	395.9	395.9	395.9	395.9	395.9	395.9	395.9	395.9	395.9
Seasonal Relatives	.609	.725	.922	.814	1.058	1.011	1.020	1.038	.967	1.136	1.315	1.387

Having computed these seasonal relatives the next question is whether or not they represent real, detectable seasonal effects. To answer this question we place the seasonal relatives on an average and range chart. All of the seasonal relatives for January are placed in one subgroup, and all of the seasonal relatives for February are placed in a second subgroup, and so on until you have 12 subgroups of two seasonal relatives each. (If you use three years of data then you would have 12 subgroups of size three.) The limits for this average and range chart are computed in the usual manner, and averages that fall outside the limits are interpreted to be *detectable seasonal effects*.

The grand average for the 12 subgroups in Figure 13.9 is 1.0000. (While the grand average for the seasonal relatives will often be close to 1.0, there is no guarantee that it must be exactly 1.0.) The average range for these 12 subgroups is 0.0169. Since we are using two years worth of data here, our subgroups are of size two. From Table 3 in the Appendix, the scaling factors for subgroups of size $n = 2$ are $A_2 = 1.880$, and $D_4 = 3.268$. Thus, we compute limits to be:

$$UAL = \bar{\bar{X}} + A_2 \bar{R} = 1.0000 + (1.880 \times 0.0169) = 1.032$$

$$LAL = \bar{\bar{X}} - A_2 \bar{R} = 1.0000 - (1.880 \times 0.0169) = 0.968$$

$$URL = D_4 \bar{R} = 3.268 \times 0.0169 = 0.055$$

These limits are shown in Figure 13.9. With ten averages outside the limits, and with some of these falling far outside the limits, the chart indicates strong seasonality in these data.

The strength of the seasonal pattern present in the data is shown by the relationship between the running record and the limits on the average chart. If there are only two or three averages outside the limits, and if they are only slightly outside the limits, then you will not gain much by deseasonalizing the data. When there are many averages outside the limits, and when some of those averages are far outside the limits, there is strong seasonality present, and you will gain sensitivity in your analysis by deseasonalizing the data.

The range chart checks for consistency within the subgroups. Any range values that fall above the upper limit indicate that the seasonal pattern for that month may be changing from year to year, or else that a special event changed the seasonal pattern for one of the years

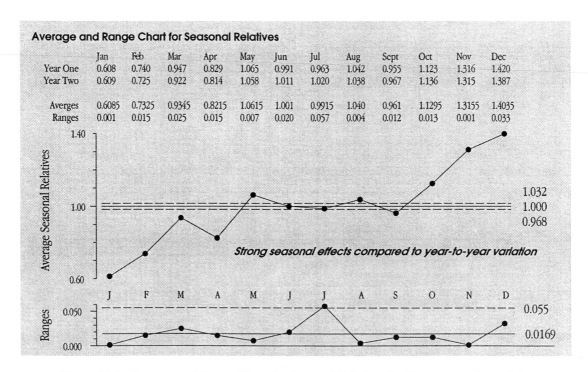

Average and Range Chart for Seasonal Relatives

	Jan	Feb	Mar	Apr	May	Jun	Jul	Aug	Sept	Oct	Nov	Dec
Year One	0.608	0.740	0.947	0.829	1.065	0.991	0.963	1.042	0.955	1.123	1.316	1.420
Year Two	0.609	0.725	0.922	0.814	1.058	1.011	1.020	1.038	0.967	1.136	1.315	1.387
Averges	0.6085	0.7325	0.9345	0.8215	1.0615	1.001	0.9915	1.040	0.961	1.1295	1.3155	1.4035
Ranges	0.001	0.015	0.025	0.015	0.007	0.020	0.057	0.004	0.012	0.013	0.001	0.033

Strong seasonal effects compared to year-to-year variation

Figure 13.9: Average and Range Chart for Seasonal Relatives for Department Store Sales

used. Here the month of July shows excessive variation from Year One to Year Two. In general, an explanation for any discrepancy between seasonal relatives should be sought. In this case, since the average seasonal relative for July is so close to 1.00, any inconsistency in our estimate of the seasonality for July will be small compared to the seasonalities for the other months. This means that any uncertainty in the estimated seasonal factor for July will not have any real impact on our seasonal adjustments, so that here we can safely ignore the inconsistency in the seasonal relatives for July.

Seasonal factors do not need to be known to high degrees of precision. Generally two or three decimal places will be sufficient. We are going to use the seasonal factors to characterize the relative inflation or deflation that is expected for each month. Rarely do we need to know this type of adjustment to more than the nearest percent. So, if the average chart shows evidence of sufficient seasonality to make it worthwhile to deseasonalize the data, we will convert the average seasonal relatives into seasonal factors by rounding them off to two (or three) decimal places.

As a check on everything having been done right, the seasonal factors should always sum up to be equal to the number of seasons. For monthly data, the sum of the 12 seasonal factors should add up to 12.00, and for quarterly data the four seasonal factors should sum up to 4.00. Since the rounded values in Table 13.8 sum to 11.99 a slight adjustment is needed. In this case we arbitrarily added 0.01 to the July seasonal factor, making it 1.00 and making the sum of all the seasonal factors equal to 12.00.

Table 13.8: Average Seasonal Relatives Converted into Seasonal Factors

	J	F	M	A	M	J	J	A	S	O	N	D
Averages	.6085	.7325	.9345	.8215	1.0615	1.001	.9915	1.040	.961	1.1295	1.3155	1.4035
Rounded	.61	.73	.93	.82	1.06	1.00	0.99	1.04	.96	1.13	1.32	1.40
Adjusted	.61	.73	.93	.82	1.06	1.00	1.00	1.04	.96	1.13	1.32	1.40

For this department store we estimate that January sales are typically 61% of the average monthly sales for the year, February sales are typically 73% of the average, March sales are typically 93% of the average, etc. These seasonal factors may be used to seasonalize forecast sales values or to deseasonalize actual sales values.

13.6 Deseasonalizing the Sales Values

When we deseasonalize our data we need to make a distinction between "baseline" values and "future" values. Baseline values will be those data that were used to compute the seasonal factors. Subsequent values will be those data that were not used in the computation of the seasonal factors. In general, the purpose of finding seasonal factors is to use them to better understand the future values, and the means by which we do this is deseasonalization. However, in addition to deseasonalizing the future values, we will also want to know whether or not the future values are consistent with the baseline values. And to do this we will need an *XmR* chart.

Therefore, the first step in analyzing the deseasonalized values will consist of placing the deseasonalized baseline values on an *XmR* chart in the usual way. Table 13.9 contains the deseasonalized baseline sales for our department store for Years One and Two. The *XmR* chart for these data is shown in Figure 13.10. The average value is 397.4 and the median moving range is 3.1.

The impact of removing the annual pattern from these data can be seen by comparing the width of the limits in Figure 13.7 on page 231 (255.6 units) with the width of the limits on the X chart of Figure 13.10 (19.5 units). By deseasonalizing these data we have removed over 90% of the month-to-month variation, resulting in a much more sensitive analysis.

Table 13.9: Deseasonalized Monthly Department Store Sales

	J	F	M	A	M	J	J	A	S	O	N	D
Yr One Monthly Sales	242.5	295.1	377.9	330.6	425.0	395.3	384.3	415.8	380.8	447.9	525.0	566.6
Seasonal Factors	0.61	0.73	0.93	0.82	1.06	1.00	1.00	1.04	0.96	1.13	1.32	1.40
Yr I Deseasonalized	397.5	404.2	406.3	403.2	400.9	395.3	384.3	399.8	396.7	396.3	397.7	404.7
mR	–	6.7	2.1	3.1	2.3	5.6	11.0	15.5	3.1	0.4	1.4	7.0
Yr Two Monthly Sales	241.0	287.2	365.0	322.1	418.8	400.2	403.7	410.9	382.8	449.8	520.7	549.1
Seasonal Factors	0.61	0.73	0.93	0.82	1.06	1.00	1.00	1.04	0.96	1.13	1.32	1.40
Yr II Deseasonalized	395.1	393.4	392.5	392.8	395.1	400.2	403.7	395.1	398.8	398.1	394.5	392.2
mR	9.6	1.7	0.9	0.3	2.3	5.1	3.5	8.6	3.7	0.7	3.6	2.3

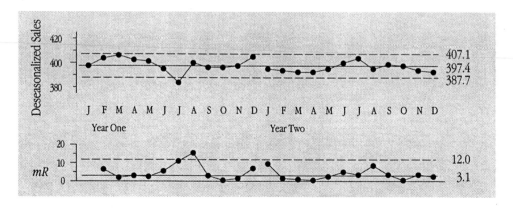

Figure 13.10: *XmR* Chart for Deseasonalized Baseline Monthly Sales

The only signal seen in Figure 13.10 is the value for July of Year One. (This signal corresponds to the range point outside the limits in Figure 13.9.) The sales for this month were exceptionally low for some reason. Since this is a historical point, it may not be possible to identify the assignable cause of this signal. However, if it is possible, we might well learn something that can be advantageous in the future.

The main reason to construct the *XmR* chart for the deseasonalized baseline values is to obtain values that can be used to construct limits for use with the deseasonalized future values. In and of itself, the chart in Figure 13.10 will not be of very great interest. The reason for this lies in an anomaly that will always be present in the deseasonalized baseline values.

When the seasonal factors are based on two years of data the pattern shown by one year will also be seen repeated, upside-down, in the other year. Figure 13.11 shows the pattern for Year One with the pattern for Year Two flipped vertically about the Grand Average of 397.4. Except for the rounding and adjusting of the seasonal factors, these two patterns would be exactly the same.

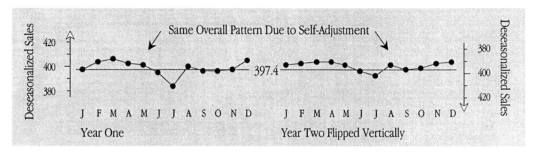

Figure 13.11: Deseasonalized Baseline Values Show the Same Pattern of Variation

This flipped pattern between Years One and Two is due to the self-adjustment that occurs when we deseasonalize the baseline values. For example, since we are dividing each of the January sales values by their average seasonal relative, one of the values will be above the grand average and the other value will be a equal distance below the grand average. The further one value is above the grand average, the further below will be the corresponding value from the other year (see Figure 13.10). The rounding and adjusting of the average seasonal relatives will disturb this equilibrium to some extent, but the overall patterns will be strikingly similar (as seen in Figure 13.11).

When three or more years are used to find the seasonal factors a more complex version of this symmetry between the baseline years will be present. In every case, this symmetry between the baseline years will make the interpretation of the *XmR* chart for the deseasonalized baseline values questionable. Since these patterns are consequences of the arithmetic of deseasonalizing the baseline data, rather than a characteristic of the underlying process, they should not be interpreted as having any meaning.

So why did we construct the *XmR* chart in Figure 13.10? In order to obtain limits to use with deseasonalized future values. However, we cannot simply use the limits from Figure 13.10. The self-adjustment that created the patterns noted above also reduces the variation of the deseasonalized baseline values.

Table 13.10: Factors for Computing Limits for Deseasonalized Future Values Based on the Deseasonalized Baseline Values

m	E_7	D_7	$\sqrt{\dfrac{m+1}{m-1}}$	E_8	D_8
2	4.607	5.660	1.732	5.447	6.694
3	3.762	4.622	1.414	4.448	5.466
4	3.434	4.219	1.291	4.060	4.990
5	3.258	4.002	1.225	3.852	4.734
6	3.147	3.867	1.183	3.721	4.573
7	3.072	3.774	1.155	3.632	4.463
8	3.016	3.706	1.134	3.566	4.382
9	2.974	3.654	1.118	3.516	4.321
10	2.941	3.613	1.106	3.477	4.273

Given an **Average** and an **Average Moving Range**
computed from the m years of *deseasonalized baseline values,*
compute limits for the *deseasonalized future values* according to:

$$UNPL = \bar{X} + 2.660 \sqrt{\frac{m+1}{m-1}}\ \bar{R} = \bar{X} + E_7\ \bar{R}$$

$$CL = \bar{X}$$

$$LNPL = \bar{X} - 2.660 \sqrt{\frac{m+1}{m-1}}\ \bar{R} = \bar{X} - E_7\ \bar{R}$$

$$URL = 3.268 \sqrt{\frac{m+1}{m-1}}\ \bar{R} = D_7\ \bar{R}$$

$$CLR = \sqrt{\frac{m+1}{m-1}}\ \bar{R}$$

Given an **Average** and a **Median Moving Range**
computed from the m years of *deseasonalized baseline values,*
compute limits for the *deseasonalized future values* according to:

$$UNPL = \bar{X} + 3.145 \sqrt{\frac{m+1}{m-1}}\ \tilde{R} = \bar{X} + E_8\ \tilde{R}$$

$$CL = \bar{X}$$

$$LNPL = \bar{X} - 3.145 \sqrt{\frac{m+1}{m-1}}\ \tilde{R} = \bar{X} + E_8\ \tilde{R}$$

$$URL = 3.865 \sqrt{\frac{m+1}{m-1}}\ \tilde{R} = D_8\ \tilde{R}$$

$$CLR = \sqrt{\frac{m+1}{m-1}}\ \tilde{R}$$

The deseasonalized future values will always show greater variation than the deseasonalized baseline values. In fact, when the seasonal factors are based on *m* years worth of data, the variation in the deseasonalized future values will be greater than the variation of the deseasonalized baseline values by a factor of:

$$\sqrt{\frac{m+1}{m-1}}$$

This inflation will change the formulas in the manner shown in Table 13.10. For the department store sales the seasonal factors were based on *m* = 2 years of data, the deseasonalized baseline values had an average of 397.4 and a median moving range of 3.1. Using these values the limits for the deseasonalized future values are *UNPL* = 414.3, *LNPL* = 380.5, *URL* = 20.75 and *CLR* = 5.37, as shown in Figure 13.12.

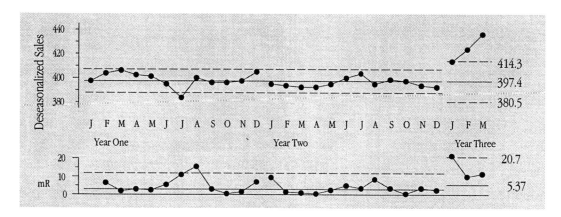

Figure 13.12: Has a Change Occurred in Year Three of Deseasonalized Monthly Sales?

What can we say about the new advertising campaign in Year Three? Did it have any impact upon sales? Should the manager continue this new approach, or drop it to save money? The deseasonalized values for the first quarter of Year Three show a detectable improvement in sales. Thus, it would seem that the change in advertising strategy was worthwhile. It is instructive to note how Figure 13.12 makes this change clear while Figures 13.6, 13.7, and 13.8 tend to obscure it.

Given that we now have evidence that Year Three is different from Years One and Two, we might want to shift our central line to reflect this change. The average of the first three deseasonalized values from Year Three is 424.5 thousand. With a central line of 424.5 thousand, and the spread of ± 16.9 thousand used in Figure 13.12, we get the limits of 407.6 thousand to 441.4 thousand shown in Figure 13.13. Thus, seasonally adjusted, the sales for the first three months of Year Three are equivalent to an average sales level of 424.5 thousand per month. Furthermore, if this new sales level is maintained, the remaining months should have seasonally adjusted sales in the region of 408 thousand to 441 thousand.

Table 13.11: Monthly Department Store Sales

	J	F	M	A	M	J	J	A	S	O	N	D
Year One	242.5	295.1	377.9	330.6	425.0	395.3	384.3	415.8	380.8	447.9	525.0	566.6
Year Two	241.0	287.2	365.0	322.1	418.8	400.2	403.7	410.9	382.8	449.8	520.7	549.1
Year Three	252.4	309.5	405.1	345.3	477.5	417.5	423.1	462.3	414.0	480.0	556.2	591.5

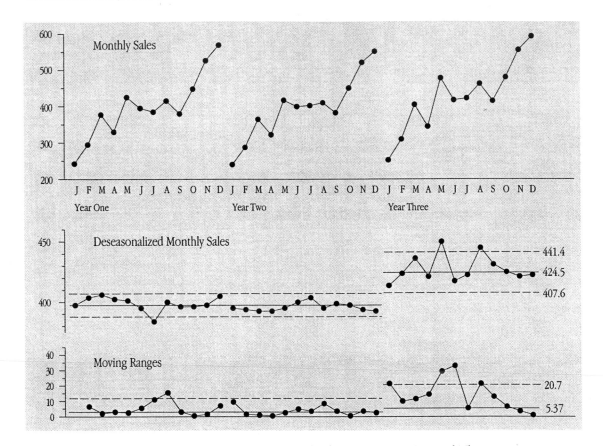

Figure 13.13: Department Store Sales for Years One, Two and Three

Perhaps the best way to present data having a strong seasonal component is a combination graph like that shown in Figure 13.13. There we combine the time-series plot of the original data with the *XmR* chart for the deseasonalized values. The time-series plot of the raw data shows both the seasonality and the actual levels of the measure, while the deseasonalized data on the *XmR* chart allows your readers to spot interesting features in the data and prompts them to ask the right questions.

In addition to the increased sales level in Year Three, both the X chart and the *mR* chart show an increased level of volatility for those sales. Using these deseasonalized monthly sales for Year Three we could use Table 2 from the Appendix to compute limits to use for forecasting Year Four.

13.7 Not All Data Show Strong Seasonality

The Department Store Sales Data in the previous section displayed strong seasonality. But not all sales data have such a consistent pattern from year to year. Here we shall return to the data shown in Table 13.2, page 225. The first two years of sales for a retail boutique, in thousands of dollars, is shown in Figure 13.14. While each year shows a general trend of increasing sales throughout the year, these values do not show the same degree of parallelism from year to year that we saw in Figure 13.6.

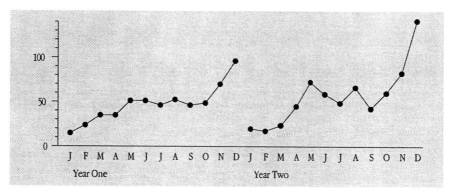

Figure 13.14: Monthly Sales for Boutique

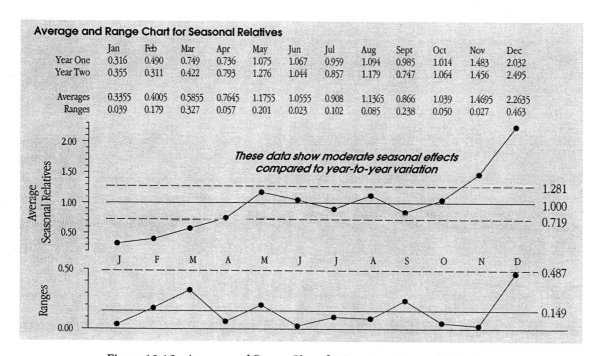

Average and Range Chart for Seasonal Relatives

	Jan	Feb	Mar	Apr	May	Jun	Jul	Aug	Sept	Oct	Nov	Dec
Year One	0.316	0.490	0.749	0.736	1.075	1.067	0.959	1.094	0.985	1.014	1.483	2.032
Year Two	0.355	0.311	0.422	0.793	1.276	1.044	0.857	1.179	0.747	1.064	1.456	2.495
Averages	0.3355	0.4005	0.5855	0.7645	1.1755	1.0555	0.908	1.1365	0.866	1.039	1.4695	2.2635
Ranges	0.039	0.179	0.327	0.057	0.201	0.023	0.102	0.085	0.238	0.050	0.027	0.463

Figure 13.15: Average and Range Chart for Boutique Seasonal Relatives

The average monthly sales for Year One was 47.533; for Year Two it was 56.592. Dividing the monthly sales by these averages we obtain the seasonal relatives shown in Figure 13.15. Even though these seasonal relatives are generally further from 100% than those in Figure 13.9, only five months show detectable seasonal effects (January, February, March, November, and December). The large amount of variation between the seasonal relatives from year to year makes it hard to detect seasonal effects here. The limits suggest that effects smaller than 28% of the average sales level are indistinguishable from routine variation. Using three years worth of data does not substantially change things. The Boutique Sales Data contain both seasonal effects and substantial amounts of noise.

The average seasonal relatives shown in Figure 13.15 are listed as the first row of Table 13.12. Since the rounded values add up to 12.02, the May and June values were adjusted down 0.01 each to give the seasonal factors shown in the third row of Table 13.12. (While only five months show a detectable seasonal effect, we will need to estimate a seasonal effect for each month and to adjust every month's values in order to use the scaling factors for computing limits given in Table 13.10.)

Table 13.12: Average Seasonal Relatives Converted into Seasonal Factors

	J	F	M	A	M	J	J	A	S	O	N	D
Averages	.3355	.4005	.5855	0.7645	1.1755	1.0555	.908	1.1365	.866	1.039	1.4695	2.2635
Rounded	.34	.40	.59	.76	1.18	1.06	.91	1.14	.87	1.04	1.47	2.26
Adjusted	.34	.40	.59	.76	1.17	1.05	.91	1.14	.87	1.04	1.47	2.26

Table 13.13: Monthly Boutique Sales and Deseasonalized Baseline Sales

	J	F	M	A	M	J	J	A	S	O	N	D
Yr I Monthly Sales	15.0	23.3	35.6	35.0	51.1	50.7	45.6	52.0	46.8	48.2	70.5	96.6
Seasonal Factors	0.34	0.40	0.59	0.76	1.17	1.05	0.91	1.14	0.87	1.04	1.47	2.26
Yr I Deseasonalized	44.1	58.3	60.3	46.1	43.7	48.3	50.1	45.6	53.8	46.3	48.0	42.7
mR		14.1	2.1	14.3	2.4	4.6	1.8	4.5	8.2	7.4	1.6	5.2
Yr II Monthly Sales	20.1	17.6	23.9	44.9	72.2	59.1	48.5	66.7	42.3	60.2	82.4	141.2
Seasonal Factors	0.34	0.40	0.59	0.76	1.17	1.05	0.91	1.14	0.87	1.04	1.47	2.26
Yr II Deseasonalized	59.1	44.0	40.5	59.1	61.7	56.3	53.3	58.5	48.6	57.9	56.1	62.5
mR	16.4	15.1	3.5	18.6	2.6	5.4	3.0	5.2	9.9	9.3	1.8	6.4

Table 13.13 gives (1) the Monthly Boutique Sales for Years One and Two, (2) the seasonal factors for these data, (3) the Deseasonalized Boutique Sales for Years One and Two, and (4) the moving ranges for these deseasonalized baseline values. The *XmR* chart for these Deseasonalized Boutique Sales for Years One and Two is included as part of Figure 13.15. The average deseasonalized baseline value is 51.87, and the median moving range is 5.2.

Once again, the self-adjustment inherent in deseasonalizing the baseline values creates the flipped pattern on the *X* chart and a repeated pattern on the *mR* chart. While these patterns make the interpretation of the *XmR* chart for the deseasonalized baseline values uninteresting, they do not interfere with our use of these values to obtain limits we can use with deseasonalized future values. To compute limits for the deseasonalized future values we return to Table 13.10: when the number of years in the baseline period is *m* = 2, we find

$E_8 = 5.447$ and $D_8 = 6.694$, thus, for the deseasonalized future values, $UNPL = 80.2$, $LNPL = 23.5$, $URL = 34.8$, and $CLR = 9.0$.

Table 13.14 contains both the Boutique Sales and the deseasonalized values for Year Three, while Figure 13.16 combines the actual sales with the *XmR* chart for the deseasonalized values for Years One, Two and Three.

The seasonal effects make it difficult to use the actual values to compare Year Three with the preceding years. However, with nine of the deseasonalized values for Year Three above the central line the increase in Year Three is easy to see. Although the deseasonalized data have wide limits, they still provide useful insights into the process.

Table 13.14: Monthly Boutique Sales and Deseasonalized Future Sales for Year Three

	J	F	M	A	M	J	J	A	S	O	N	D
Yr III Monthly Sales	19.0	28.8	35.6	48.1	63.8	49.3	45.6	52.2	46.1	72.9	98.4	122.1
Seasonal Factors	*0.34*	*0.40*	*0.59*	*0.76*	*1.17*	*1.05*	*0.91*	*1.14*	*0.87*	*1.04*	*1.47*	*2.26*
Yr I Deseasonalized	55.9	72.0	60.3	63.3	54.5	47.0	50.1	45.8	53.0	70.1	66.9	54.0
mR	6.6	16.1	11.7	3.0	8.8	7.6	3.2	4.3	7.2	17.1	3.2	12.9

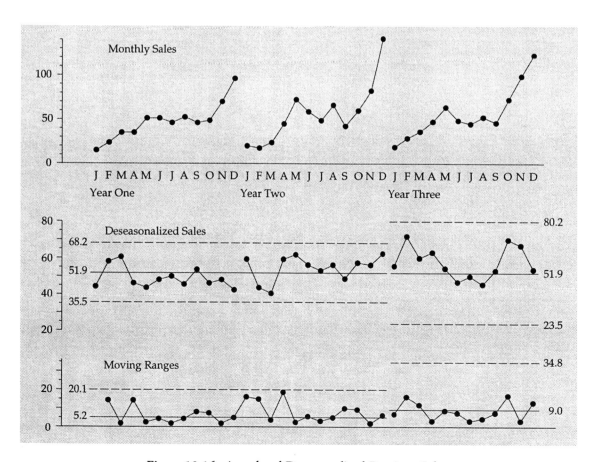

Figure 13.16: Actual and Deseasonalized Boutique Sales

So how can the manager of the boutique track his sales in the face of seasonality and noise? While it helps to remove the seasonality, he still has the problem of making sense of the current values in spite of the noise. When the data are noisy, a year-long moving average will allow you to smooth out both seasonal effects and noise so that you can see the underlying trend. The data of Figure 13.16 were shown with a twelve-period moving average in Figure 13.3. There the moving average made the gradual upward trend in sales visible. Given data that contain both a substantial seasonal component and considerable noise, the annual moving average will show the underlying trend better than the deseasonalized data.

13.8 The Appliance Store Data

The Appliance Store Sales Data will serve as an example of data where seasonal effects are weak and noise is substantial.

Table 13.15: Monthly Appliance Store Sales

Year	J	F	M	A	M	J	J	A	S	O	N	D	Average
One	86.9	78.3	97.2	77.3	113.5	99.5	75.0	81.8	113.4	122.3	74.4	80.4	91.67
Two	72.3	78.1	91.5	91.7	141.5	113.2	107.0	96.7	99.1	71.8	78.4	46.5	90.65
Three	82.0	117.1	98.0	85.5	105.6	69.8	63.7	81.9	78.8	96.1	70.1	58.9	83.96

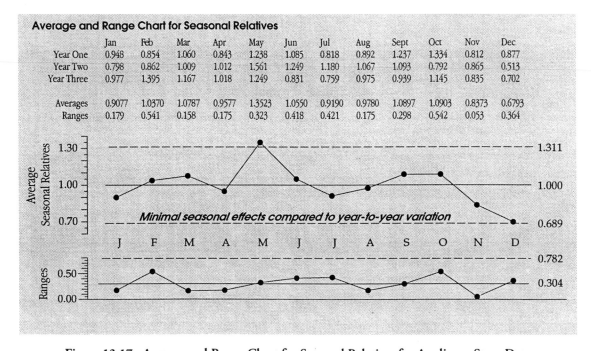

Figure 13.17: Average and Range Chart for Seasonal Relatives for Appliance Store Data

Table 13.16: 12-Period Moving Averages for the Appliance Store Sales

Year	J	F	M	A	M	J	J	A	S	O	N	D
One												91.7
Two	90.5	90.4	90.0	91.1	93.5	94.6	97.3	98.5	97.4	93.1	93.5	90.7
Three	91.5	94.7	95.3	94.7	91.7	88.1	84.5	83.3	81.6	83.6	82.9	84.0

The limits in Figure 13.17 show that a seasonal effect would have to be bigger than ± 31% in order to be detectable above the noise present in these data. These data contain weak seasonal effects and a lot of noise. In fact, only one month has a detectable seasonal effect. Therefore, the seasonal adjustment of the data in Table 13.15 would effectively change only 3 of the 36 values by any appreciable amount while shuffling the other 33 values around. Thus, deseasonalization will not clarify things in this case.

On the other hand, the 12-period moving average shows the overall trend for these sales data. Figure 13.18 contains both the individual values and the 12-period moving average for this store. The 12-period moving average shows that the appliance store sales have declined slightly over this three-year period.

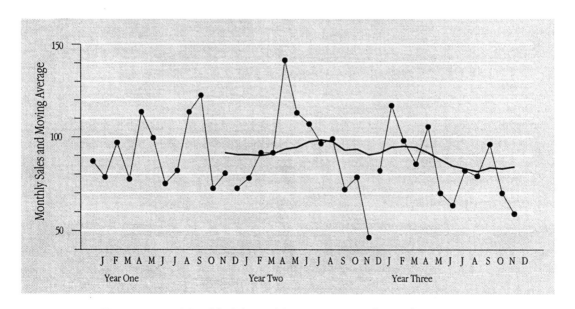

Figure 13.18: Monthly Sales and Moving Average for Appliance Store

Unless the seasonal components are substantially greater than the year-to-year variation in the seasonal relatives you will gain little by deseasonalizing the data. The average and range chart uses the calculations that are part of finding the seasonal effects to allow you to assess this aspect of your data.

13.9 The Claims Per Day Data

The claims processing division of a large health insurance company kept track of its productivity by dividing the number of claims processed each month by the total number of man-days worked that month. This ratio was known as "Claims Per Day" and was used, along with similar measures from other divisions, to evaluate and rank the division managers. The Claims Per Day values are shown in Figure 13.19. These values are aggregate values based upon the data from the eight regional offices.

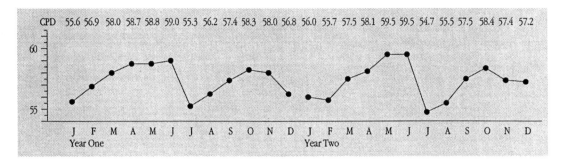

Figure 13.19: Claims Per Day Values for Years One and Two

The relative parallelism between these two years suggests that strong seasonal effects are present in these data. The managers had an explanation for this seasonality—it was said to be a consequence of variable staffing in response to the seasonal variation in claims. While there was a core of full-time personnel who processed claims, there was another group of

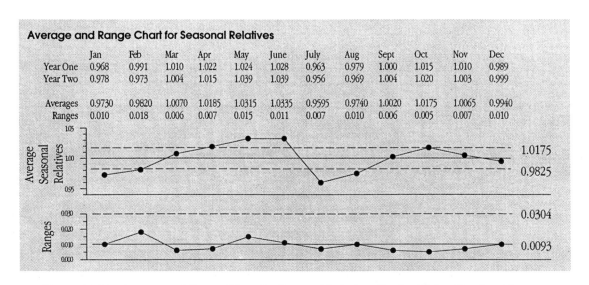

Average and Range Chart for Seasonal Relatives

	Jan	Feb	Mar	Apr	May	June	July	Aug	Sept	Oct	Nov	Dec
Year One	0.968	0.991	1.010	1.022	1.024	1.028	0.963	0.979	1.000	1.015	1.010	0.989
Year Two	0.978	0.973	1.004	1.015	1.039	1.039	0.956	0.969	1.004	1.020	1.003	0.999
Averages	0.9730	0.9820	1.0070	1.0185	1.0315	1.0335	0.9595	0.9740	1.0020	1.0175	1.0065	0.9940
Ranges	0.010	0.018	0.006	0.007	0.015	0.011	0.007	0.010	0.006	0.005	0.007	0.010

Figure 13.20: Average and Range Chart for Seasonal Relatives for the Claims Per Day Data

personnel who were used on a part-time basis to help when the number of claims went up in the winter and when regular personnel were on vacation in the summer. Since the part-time personnel were not as efficient as the full-time personnel, the productivity measure suffered when they were used. The seasonal relatives for these two years are shown on the average and range chart in Figure 13.20. As can be seen there, seven or eight months can be said to have detectable seasonal effects.

The average seasonal relatives are converted into seasonal factors in Table 13.17. The sum of the rounded values is 11.99, so December's value was rounded up to 1.00.

Table 13.17: Converting Average Seasonal Relatives into Seasonals

	J	F	M	A	M	J	J	A	S	O	N	D
Averages	0.9730	0.9820	1.0070	1.0185	1.0315	1.0335	0.9595	0.9740	1.002	1.0175	1.0065	0.9940
Rounded	0.97	0.98	1.01	1.02	1.03	1.03	0.96	0.97	1.00	1.02	1.01	0.99
Seasonals	0.97	0.98	1.01	1.02	1.03	1.03	0.96	0.97	1.00	1.02	1.01	1.00

Table 13.18: Claims Per Day Values and Deseasonalized Baseline Values

	J	F	M	A	M	J	J	A	S	O	N	D
Year One	55.6	56.9	58.0	58.7	58.8	59.0	55.3	56.2	57.4	58.3	58.0	56.8
Seasonals	*0.97*	*0.98*	*1.01*	*1.02*	*1.03*	*1.03*	*0.96*	*0.97*	*1.00*	*1.02*	*1.01*	*1.00*
Yr I Deseason.	57.3	58.1	57.4	57.5	57.1	57.3	57.6	57.9	57.4	57.2	57.4	56.8
mR		0.8	0.7	0.1	0.4	0.2	0.3	0.3	0.5	0.2	0.2	0.6
Year Two	56.0	55.7	57.5	58.1	59.5	59.5	54.7	55.5	57.5	58.4	57.4	57.2
Seasonals	*0.97*	*0.98*	*1.01*	*1.02*	*1.03*	*1.03*	*0.96*	*0.97*	*1.00*	*1.02*	*1.01*	*1.00*
Yr II Deseason.	57.7	56.8	56.9	57.0	57.8	57.8	57.0	57.2	57.5	57.3	56.8	57.2
mR	0.9	0.9	0.1	0.1	0.8	0.0	0.8	0.2	0.3	0.2	0.5	0.4

The deseasonalized baseline values shown in Table 13.18 have an average of 57.34 and a median moving range of 0.30. The XmR chart for the deseasonalized baseline values is shown as part of Figure 13.21. Limits for deseasonalized future values are: $UNPL = 58.97$, $LNPL = 55.71$, $URL = 2.01$, and $CLR = 0.52$.

The Claims Per Day values for Year Three and the deseasonalized future values are shown in Table 13.19.

Table 13.19: Claims Per Day Values and Deseasonalized Future Values for Year Three

	J	F	M	A	M	J	J	A	S	O	N	D
Year Three	55.4	54.7	56.8	58.5	58.4	57.6	54.4	54.0	55.7	57.1	56.8	55.6
Seasonals	*0.97*	*0.98*	*1.01*	*1.02*	*1.03*	*1.03*	*0.96*	*0.97*	*1.00*	*1.02*	*1.01*	*1.00*
Yr III Deseason.	57.1	55.8	56.2	57.4	56.7	55.9	56.7	55.7	55.7	56.0	56.2	55.6
mR	0.1	1.3	0.4	1.1	0.7	0.8	0.7	1.0	0.0	0.3	0.3	0.6

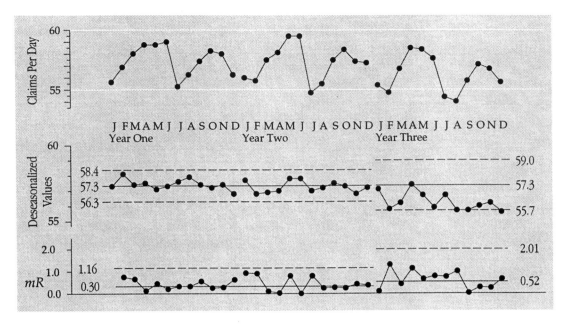

Figure 13.21: Claims Per Day Values and *XmR* Chart for Years One, Two and Three

The top portion of Figure 13.21 shows the time series for Claims Per Day. These are the actual values without any seasonal adjustment. While the first three values for Year Three appear to be a little low, it is not clear from the actual values if there has been a change in productivity.

However, the X chart for the deseasonalized future values shows evidence of a change by March of Year Three (two successive points in the outer one-third of the limits on an X chart is another type of run near the limits). While the productivity for April was back up to the previous average, it is the only month in Year Three that exceeded that average. The remainder of Year Three shows an overall decline in productivity, with the last five months hugging the lower limit. Something has changed for the worse, and the X chart shows this change more clearly than the actual values.

The only explanation for the lower productivity in Year Three that they could find was the implementation of new corporate policies and procedures in late January. While we might expect a temporary dip associated with a learning curve following such a change, Figure 13.21 shows a sustained drop in productivity. In other words, the "improvements" put in place at the beginning of Year Three actually made things worse.

So what limits should we now use for Year Four? Since these data are report-card data it makes sense to revise the limits to reflect the current process behavior. To this end we shall use the deseasonalized values from Year Three to compute limits directly. The average for these values is 56.25, while the average moving range is 0.608. Using the regular formulas from Table 2 in the Appendix these values give Natural Process Limits of 57.87 and 54.63, and an Upper Range Limit of 1.99. These limits are shown in Figure 13.22.

Since the deseasonalized values for Year Three all fall within these limits, we might use these limits to forecast Year Four. Namely, if they do not change things for the better, and if they do not change things for the worse, the claim processing division should expect to average about 56 claims per day per operator during Year Four. To expect the process to do better than this is unrealistic. Improvement does not tend to happen spontaneously.

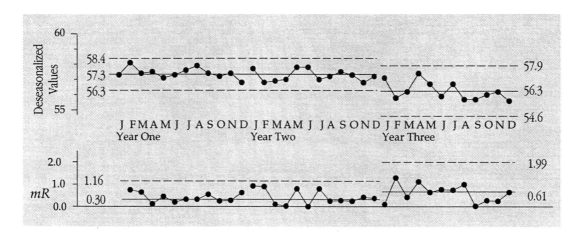

Figure 13.22: *XmR* Chart for Deseasonalized Claims Per Day for Years One, Two and Three

Following the drop in productivity in Year Three, the CEO of this health insurance company decided that they needed to take action to remedy things—it was time to reengineer the whole organization. A thorough reorganization was undertaken, along with a thinning of the ranks of mid-level managers. Goals were set for each area of operations, and Year Four was declared to be the year of the turn-around. Everyone knew that it was just a matter of time until the benefits of the reshuffling became evident.

The claim processing division was given a "stretch goal" of 60 claims per day. Since the average in Year Three was about 56 claims per day, they were expecting the reorganization to yield an increase of about 4 claims per day.

Table 13.20 shows the Claims Per Day values for Year Four, along with the deseasonalized values. These values are shown in a composite running record and *XmR* chart in Figure 13.23 on the following page.

Table 13.20: Claims Per Day Values and Deseasonalized CPD Values

	J	F	M	A	M	J	J	A	S	O	N	D
Year 4	51.9	52.7	55.4	54.7	54.1	54.1	50.6	50.5	51.6	51.3	51.0	51.8
Seasonals	0.97	0.98	1.01	1.02	1.03	1.03	0.96	0.97	1.00	1.02	1.01	1.00
Deseas.	53.5	53.8	54.9	53.6	52.5	52.5	52.7	52.1	51.6	50.3	50.5	51.8
mR	2.1	0.3	1.1	1.2	1.1	0.0	0.2	0.6	0.5	1.3	0.2	1.3

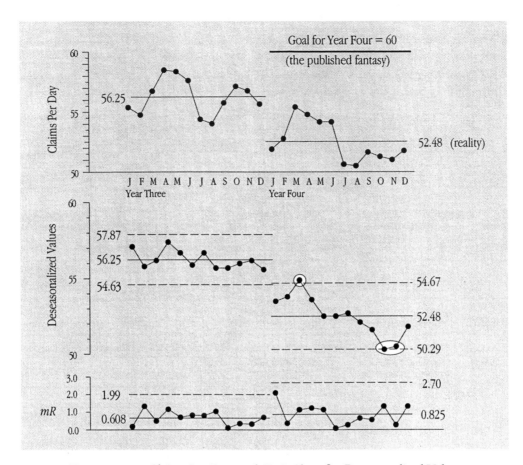

Figure 13.23: Claims Per Day, and *XmR* Chart for Deseasonalized Values

The published fantasy was that the productivity would go up about four units with the new system. The reality was that the productivity went down about four units—which is the usual result of wishful thinking. This drop in productivity at the beginning of Year Four can be seen in every portion of Figure 13.23. It is beyond question. The only real question is what happened? Since the reorganization occurred in January of Year Four, it is the logical explanation for the overall drop in productivity. Moreover, the deseasonalized values also show signals of changes in productivity during Year Four.

Whenever goals or targets are proposed the question that should always be asked is, "By what method?" The setting of goals or targets is no substitute for studying the process to discover how to improve it by removing assignable causes of excessive variation.

Goals, targets, and reorganizations are frequently signs of desperation—admissions that managers do not have a clue as to what to do to change things for the better. They just roll the dice and hope things will improve. Process behavior charts provide an alternative to this everlasting game of chance. They give a way of learning about processes and systems so that we can improve them. They identify the opportunities for improvement, and they identify processes that are operating up to their potential. Knowing the difference is crucial. Not knowing the difference is a disaster.

Those who sponsor improvements often come to believe their own claims. The best antidote to this form of self-delusion is to listen to the Voice of the Process.

In the absence of effective ways of analyzing the data you may be subject to being misled by unsubstantiated claims of improvement. The best antidote to this form of misinformation is to listen to the Voice of the Process.

Without the Voice of the Process, it's just an opinion—and that opinion is likely to be based upon wishful thinking. And that is why, without process behavior charts, you are doomed to live and work in dreamland.

13.10 Working with Seasonal Data

When you suspect that your data contains seasonal patterns you may use the list below as a step-by-step guide on how to remove the seasonal effects.

1. Plot your data in a running record. If a repeating pattern is apparent, then go to Step 2. Otherwise go to Step 6.

2. Use a few complete cycles of the seasonal pattern to obtain seasonal relatives.

3. Place seasonal relatives on an average and range chart where each subgroup represents a single "season." Points outside the limits on the average chart will indicate detectable seasonal effects, while points far outside these limits will denote strong seasonal effects. If data only show weak seasonality then go to Step 6.

4. Estimate the seasonal factors for every period. The seasonal factors for a five-day cycle must sum to 5; for a seven-day cycle they must sum to 7. Quarterly seasonals must sum to 4, while monthly seasonals must sum to 12.

5. Deseasonalize baseline and future values by dividing each value by the seasonal factor for that period. Place these deseasonalized baseline values on an *XmR* chart. Use these values to compute limits for deseasonalized future values according to Table 13.10. Interpret the chart for deseasonalized future values in the usual manner.

6. Place the individual values on an *XmR* chart. If this chart is useful then interpret it in the usual way. If the limits on the *X* chart are so wide that they do not provide any useful information about your process (except the fact that noise is dominant), go to Step 7.

7. When noise dominates a time series it essentially becomes a report card on the past. In this case it can still be helpful to plot a running record of the individual values with a year-long moving average superimposed to show the underlying trends.

To help you with the judgment about the possibility of seasonal patterns in your data the following figures are provided. They are a recap of the figures in this and previous chapters. In general, whenever a recurring pattern exists there is a possibility of seasonality. If the shape of the pattern is changing from cycle to cycle the seasonality is likely to be moderate. If the shape of the pattern persists then the seasonality will be strong.

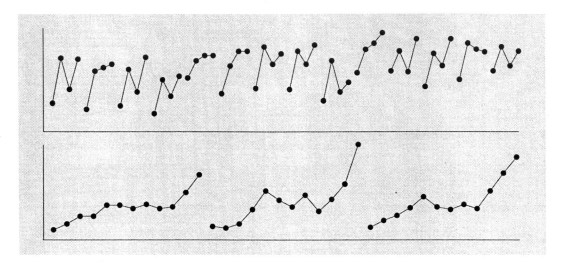

Figure 13.24: Some Time Series Which Display Moderate Seasonality

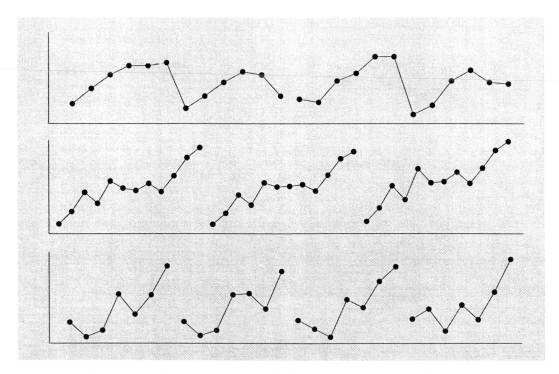

Figure 13.25: Some Time Series Which Display Strong Seasonal Patterns

13.11 Exercises

EXERCISE 13.1

Three years worth of quarterly sales data are shown in Table 13.21. Place the seasonal relatives on an Average and Range chart. Do these data display detectable seasonality?

Table 13.21: Monthly Sales

Year	I	II	III	IV	Average
One	146	139	135	140	140.0
Two	150	141	139	142	143.0
Three	153	143	141	145	145.5

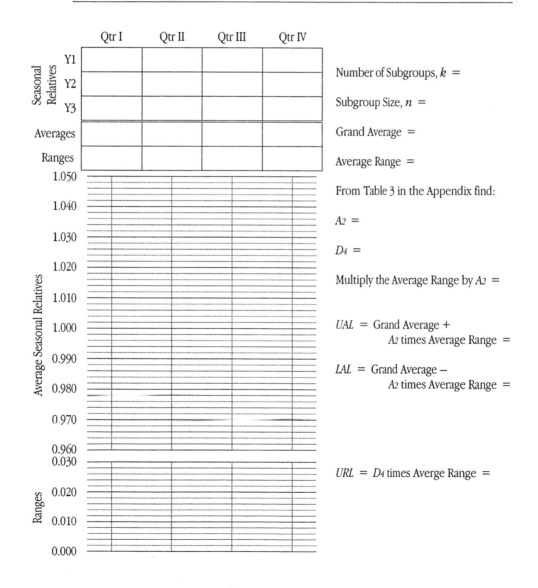

Number of Subgroups, k =

Subgroup Size, n =

Grand Average =

Average Range =

From Table 3 in the Appendix find:

A_2 =

D_4 =

Multiply the Average Range by A_2 =

UAL = Grand Average +
$\qquad$ A_2 times Average Range =

LAL = Grand Average −
$\qquad$ A_2 times Average Range =

URL = D_4 times Averge Range =

EXERCISE 13.2

Estimate the seasonal factors (to two decimal places) for each quarter for the sales data in Exercise 13.1, then compute the deseasonalized baseline values and place them on an *XmR* chart.

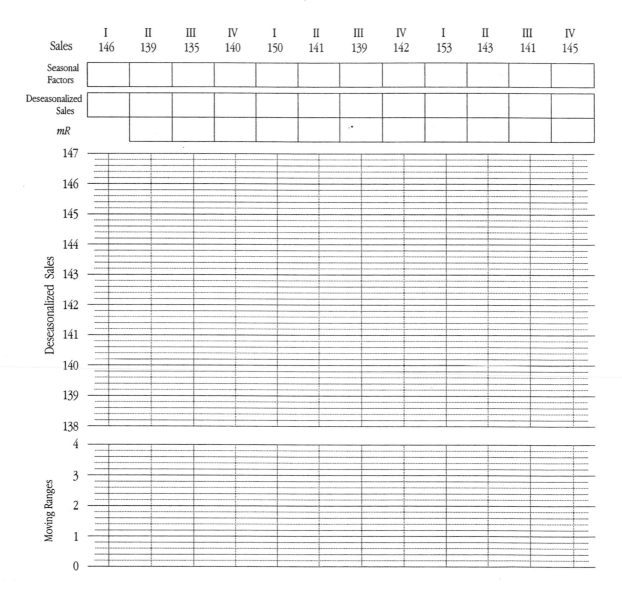

	I	II	III	IV	I	II	III	IV	I	II	III	IV
Sales	146	139	135	140	150	141	139	142	153	143	141	145
Seasonal Factors												
Deseasonalized Sales												
mR												

The signals on this chart reveal something about the sales data. What is it?

Using the averages for Years 1 & 3, what would you estimate the average for Year Four to be?

What would you estimate the average for Year Five to be?

EXERCISE 13.3

1. Use your estimated averages for Years Four and Five with the Average Moving Range from Exercise 13.2, along with Table 13.10, to obtain limits for the Year Four and Year Five deseasonalized future values.
2. The sales for Years Four and Five are shown below. Deseasonalize these values and plot these deseasonalized future values on the X chart.

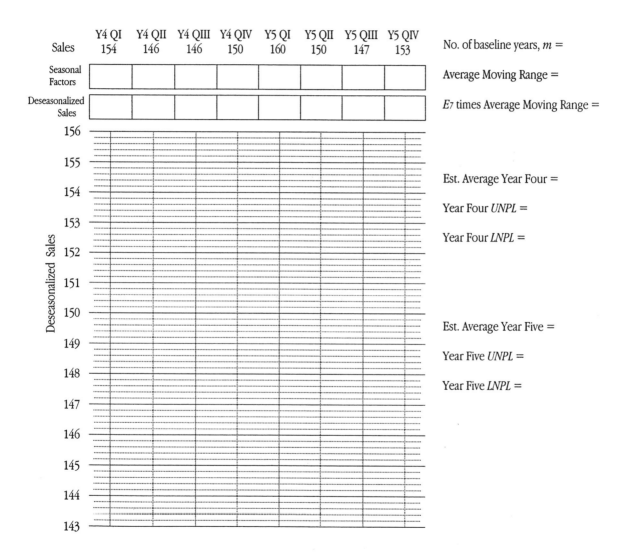

No. of baseline years, m =

Average Moving Range =

E_7 times Average Moving Range =

Est. Average Year Four =

Year Four *UNPL* =

Year Four *LNPL* =

Est. Average Year Five =

Year Five *UNPL* =

Year Five *LNPL* =

EXERCISE 13.4 Compute a four-period moving average for the sales data:

	Year	Qtr	Sales	Sums	Averages
1	One	I	146		
2		II	139		
3		III	135		
4		IV	140	_____	_____
5	Two	I	150	_____	_____
6		II	141	_____	_____
7		III	139	_____	_____
8		IV	142	_____	_____
9	Three	I	153	_____	_____
10		II	143	_____	_____
11		III	141	_____	_____
12		IV	145	_____	_____
13	Four	I	154	_____	_____
14		II	146	_____	_____
15		III	146	_____	_____
16		IV	150	_____	_____
17	Five	I	160	_____	_____
18		II	150	_____	_____
19		III	147	_____	_____
20		IV	153	_____	_____

Plot both the sales values and the moving averages below.

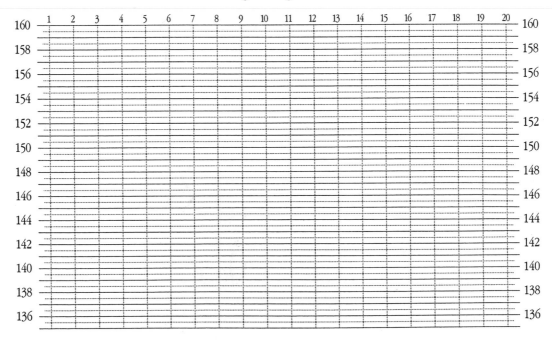